Praise for *Everyone Has a Plan Until They Get Punched in the Face*

Lucas has the personality that instantly lifts the mood of everyone around him. He has the ability to motivate without trying. He can help you find the story behind your company and what makes you different from those around you. This book encompasses all of his combined tools and energy, rolled into something you can keep with you at all times. When we first started working with Lucas, he helped identify and convey what makes us unique, and knowing this has created drastic improvements in our client relationships and culture.

Richard Brown, GM and Vice President of The BoxMaker

Everyone Has a Plan Until They Get Punched in the Face is a must-read for those looking to define their life dreams and make them a reality. The book not only helps to hold you accountable to your dreams but also enables readers to anticipate the inevitable obstacles that will be faced along the way. Author Lucas Mack uses real-life struggles that he's faced as an entrepreneur, which I found myself relating to. This book is a great inspiration not only to business owners but to anybody looking to fulfill their life dreams.

Michael Brandt, Senior Brand Strategist
for Capital One and Entrepreneur

Lucas Mack is an expert at story. He lives his story every day and delivers on his WHY: "freeing people through story." I have personally observed and experienced this as a peer, client, and friend. VICTORY!

Richard Brune, Partner at One Accord Partners, Inc.

I am excited about the impact this book will have on the many lives who seek to be great. Certainly Lucas Mack continues to demonstrate strong communication and leadership, drafting a message we all need to hear and be encouraged by.

Josh Dunn, President of Premier Media Group

Lucas Mack writes that 'inspired people inspire people,' and it's evident that this book is written from a place of gritty, authentic inspiration. Quite wonderfully, Lucas can't separate his passion for helping you develop your story because in doing so, he is fulfilling his own story.

Dr. Mark Adams, Founder of ONVO Whole Body Health

Lucas Mack has qualities you rarely find in a person but are always seeking. When you read *Everyone Has a Plan Until They Get Punched in the Face*, you will get the honesty, real-world application, and the guidance you've been seeking to help you develop YOUR story and live the life you want to lead.

Marshall Macias, Serial Entrepreneur
and Business Consultant

People spend years chasing their dreams blindly, based solely on what they see others doing on television or in the mainstream media. Lucas Mack is dead-on with his techniques for achieving satisfaction in life, without wasting time. Lucas Mack is a true leader who knows how to motivate and inspire others.

James Keith, Assistant News Director, KABB-TV

Lucas Mack is gifted at helping others tell their story. For Lucas's business clients, this translates into differentiation that matters, increasing revenue and profits. If you want to fast-track your company to dramatically higher business success, then read and profit from *Everyone Has a Plan Until They Get Punched in the Face.* You'll be glad you did!

Earl Bell, Author, *Winning in Baseball and Business*

EVERYONE HAS
A PLAN
UNTIL THEY GET
PUNCHED
IN THE FACE

EVERYONE HAS
A PLAN
UNTIL THEY GET
PUNCHED
IN THE FACE

HOW TO DEVELOP YOUR STORY
AND ACHIEVE YOUR DREAMS

LUCAS MACK

ENTREPRENEUR
PUBLISHING

For permission requests, please address
Entrepreneur Publishing
PO Box 2222
Poulsbo, WA 98370

Published 2014 by Entrepreneur Publishing
Printed in the United States of America

18 17 16 15 14   1 2 3 4 5

ISBN 978-1-936672-69-1

Library of Congress Control Number: 2014931321

CONTENTS

ACKNOWLEDGEMENTS

Writing this book has been a journey, and one that I didn't take on my own. I'd like to first thank my precious wife for putting up with my late nights and early mornings away as I worked on this. I'd like to thank the three men on my advisory board who encouraged me to write this book and stuck with me through the highs and lows of the past three years: Earl Bell, Richard Brune, and Mark Walters. Thanks to Marshall Macias, Cass Holloway, and Trey Schorr for the editing work. A big thank you to Andrea Ryder for working with me to fine-tune my thoughts and put them down on paper. Thank you, Katy Hart, for the amazing book cover design.

Thank you to all my clients who have continued to shape my story as I work on shaping yours. I am humbled and honored to have such amazing people in my life, and I hope this book reflects your contribution to my life. Victory!

INTRODUCTION

Everyone has a dream. Each of us has a vision, goal, or ideal for the future. But what is a dream (figuratively speaking, of course)? The best definition of a dream I have come up with thus far is that it is a presumed state of happiness. A dream is something you hope to achieve. However, too often we are afraid to admit our dream or vision because we are mistaken in thinking we need to have these big, Disney dreams. The truth is, a dream can be anything, big or small, and we can have multiple dreams for ourselves. A dream motivates you to get out of bed in the morning and influences the decisions you make. Yet often we are afraid of being judged that our dream is "too small" or "not good enough." In this way we wander through life thinking we don't have a dream, or we deny that we do. If you are one of those people, then I want to say this to you right now: You do have a dream. And that dream is valid and worth pursuing.

This book's intention is to make you successful in this pursuit. I want to give you the tools and understanding to ensure you will be able to withstand the hits that will inevitably occur on the way to achieving your dreams. I have witnessed and personally experienced being knocked down, deflated, and completely demoralized when my vision didn't work out the way I had planned. When this happens, we are conditioned to retreat back to a place in our life that is safe and comfortable. We develop this mentality of, "Why should I pursue that again after the last terrible experience?" This thinking too easily consumes us and renders us weak, numb, and trapped by the confines of what we *think* we know and what we *think* we can do. But guess what? Everything you believe you know has been told to you by someone else who heard it from someone else, and so on. There is an author of every action, because there is an author of every belief. Someone has made a decision somewhere that affects the experience we have, and when we don't stop to question the author of our beliefs that lead to our actions, we fall into a perpetuating cycle of assumption and complacency. I believe, though, that deep down everyone wants to leave that place, as comfortable as it may feel.

My solution to break this cycle is simple: story. I believe that only when you *fully* develop your own unique story will you be empowered to think critically and independently in a way that will give you the freedom to achieve your dreams, whatever they may be. Together, we will achieve Victory (yes, with a capital *V*).

The rest of this book will address the simple guidelines to follow and steps to take in order to be victorious and eliminate the possibility of failure. I want to share with you how to rally your defenses and never get caught off-guard, no matter how many right hooks or uppercuts come your way.

1

THE TIME TO
BE FREE IS NOW

STO•RY — N.
1 TRUTH

Up until now, you have never had real control over your life. Don't get me wrong, you have made decisions that have led to outcomes, but you only navigated inside the confines of a presumed state of mind. Without questioning why you believe what you believe and who was the original author of what you believe, you've operated under false pretenses that you are "free." But in reality, you are not. Without asking the fundamental questions that make up your story, you are like a person who jumps into a river and has no control to navigate against the current. You simply get swept downstream under the power of a preconditioned force. Even when you use your energy to stay afloat, you are operating under a power you didn't choose for yourself. This is exactly how most people live their lives. Don't let yourself get swept up in the current without first knowing why you want to jump in and where you want to go.

The only way to free yourself from your present state and become empowered to make decisions that will result in fulfilling your dream is when you develop your story. It's time to stop assuming you are the author of everything you believe and start asking the right questions, so you'll know you are. Until you question your current state of being and how you got where you are, you will not achieve your dream. The good news is everyone starts out in the same boat, and there is hope to control your own life. It begins with figuring out why you believe what you believe. Figuring that out will enable you to take control of your own life and truly be free—free to make informed decisions, free to choose what to believe, and free to know why. All this leads to freedom from assumption, your current state of being.

In this book I'm going to teach you how to develop your story, define your audience, and then distribute your story to your audience in order to achieve your dream. It's never too late to start, so let the journey begin.

FIRST STEP: WRITE IT DOWN

"You shall know the truth, and the truth shall make you free." This saying is not just a metaphor; I have experienced it firsthand. What is truth, one may ask. Truth in the context of this book is your story. The only way to discover your own personal story is to honestly answer through self reflection the five questions: *Who, What,*

When, Where, and *Why.* These are the five questions that make a story. The truth, the answer to each of these questions, already exists, but you need to ask them for yourself to discover the answers. Truth and story are synonyms. Discover truth through story, and discover story through truth.

Developing your story is important because when you discover what you believe, which is the answer to your *why,* then you'll have a passion that will help you sustain the hits *when* (not *if*) they come. By discovering your *who, what, when,* and *where,* you'll be able to avoid the hits. Together, these answers make up your story. Together, they will make you unbreakable.

Getting hit with obstacles shouldn't derail us. In fact, it shouldn't even surprise us. Obstacles are meant to be overcome. That's what an obstacle is. If you know your unique story and believe in your *why,* then nothing can stop you from achieving your dreams. Developing your story to avoid the hits is crucial.

In this quote from one of my favorite movies, *Rocky Balboa,* Rocky does a great job explaining the reality of this:

Let me tell you something you already know. The world ain't all sunshine and rainbows. It's a very mean and nasty place, and I don't care how tough you are, it will beat you to your knees and keep you there permanently if you let it. You, me, or nobody is gonna hit as hard as life.

But it ain't about how hard you hit; it's about how hard you can get hit and keep moving forward. How much you can take and keep moving forward. That's how winning is done!

So how do you begin developing your story? First, write out the five questions that make a story: *who, what, when, where,* and *why*. Fully answer each of these questions to make sure you know your complete story. Grab a pen and paper, spend some time thinking about the answers, and start writing. Think hard about each question, and don't take the first answer that comes to mind. Keep asking the questions until you strip back all the voices from others and self-talk and are left with just the unvarnished truth. When you do this, I'm guessing you'll easily state *who* you are, *when* you started, and *where* you're headed. Answering the *what* may be trickier, but the question that will likely present the biggest challenge for you is the *why*.

Here is my advice: your *why* should be more than a motive. It is your belief statement, *why* you do what you do. *Why* thinking goes well beyond your current circumstances and sits akin to your dream, your vision. It's the reason you wake up every morning and do what you love to do. It is what makes you uniquely different from everyone else. Here is a formula I created that will help you develop your *why* statement:

Only when *x* can *y*, which *z*.

The variable y is your desired outcome. The variable z is the answer to how your audience will benefit. The variable x is the answer to your *why*, which everything you do is funneled through. For instance, I believe only when you develop your authentic story (x) can you be free to fulfill your dream (y), which inspires others to do the same (z). My *why* is freeing people through story.

When answering *why*, if you stated, "to make money," you're not alone. Money is the most common answer I hear, but the fact is that this is simply not true. Making money is a byproduct of what you do. For most people, if they got paid an exuberant amount of money to do what they do for a living, they would continue to work just as hard, because their passion is not fueled by money. You could be doing a number of different jobs or careers that could bring you more money, but if you like your job, you're not doing it for the money. If you are unhappy with your current career choice, it's time to develop your story and take the steps toward experiencing freedom.

You will know your true *why* when you discover what makes you passionate about what you do and why others should care. Finding out your *why* is just as much about figuring out who you are as it is about who you are not. When you are able to answer your *why*, you'll notice that you will begin to attract the right kind of people around you, both personally and professionally. With the right kind of people surrounding you, you'll have others to lean on during the hard times, which will help motivate you to continue on the journey toward achieving your dream.

Everyone has a plan until they get punched in the face. But those who have a fully developed story and get hit will continue on the path to achieving their dream because they have clearly figured out *why* they are doing what they're doing. They will keep their eyes on the end goal and accept the means along the way. No one is perfect, but if you're willing to accept and overcome the mistakes you will surely make on the journey to achieving your vision, then you can prepare yourself for anything. Don't be afraid of getting hit.

INSPIRED PEOPLE, INSPIRE PEOPLE

The only thing that sets you apart in life is your story, and until you know your story, you'll never be free to pursue your vision with clarity and passion. I look around and see a world of people lacking clarity and a reason for action. But that can change, and the time for change is now. It's not that people don't have passion; it's just that we have never been properly taught how to find it, fuel it, or act on it.

I like to look to history for examples of amazing men and women who have made tremendous change in the world around them. As my dad always told me growing up, "Inspired people inspire people." If history has shown us anything, it is this: when inspired people share their passion with others, people follow and lives are changed forever. The pages of human history are filled with men and women who inspired and led people to strive for something greater, whether it was in business, politics, or religion. A well-developed story is inspiring—it is the best reason you can give to get someone to join you in your cause. Story is the purest form of one's truth, making it irrefutable and worthy of pursuing.

Social media aficionado and brand storyteller Jon Thomas wrote in his article "7 Reasons Storytelling is Important,"

Stories produce experiences, and experiences leave lasting impressions. They go far deeper than facts, figures, or features. And by creating a story-based experience, you cause your audiences to walk away with an impression of your brand that doesn't rest on the precarious edges of their minds but sits deep in their hearts.

As Thomas says, connecting with the heart is the whole point of story. Whether you are inspired and fueled by passion from discovering your story or your audience is inspired when they hear your story, connecting with the heart and mind is of the utmost importance when conveying a message.

History has given us plenty of heroic examples of people

who inspire us because they shared their story. One of my personal favorites is Daniel "Rudy" Ruettiger, who was told he was too small to play football, but through his sheer determination and passion, he realized his dream of playing football for Notre Dame. Standing only 5'8" and weighing 185 pounds, Rudy's heart yearned to play football for the Fighting Irish. He believed that the passion inside someone and not their size should determine their future.

Usually the stories that inspire us, like Rudy's, revolve around the underdog—people who dared to challenge the status quo and in turn changed the world around them. Anyone who faces adversity becomes an underdog. If you have a dream, then guess what, you're already an underdog because all the odds are stacked against you. But that means you've got something to prove. It means that you can change the status quo if you believe the way things are isn't how they should stay.

Another great example of someone who knew his story and shared it with others to bring about the change he sought was the character William Wallace from the movie *Braveheart*. In the film, the majority of Scottish people despised British tyranny, but only one man was able to inspire them to finally, once and for all, be rid of the tyranny that kept them from being free. William Wallace was that man, and as he stated, "Every man dies. Not every man really lives." He believed that all people are born free and should live free to choose for themselves the life they want to live, in harmony with their neighbor. His intense belief that all men should live free combined with his ability to articulate that to others was what united the Scottish people to fight with passion and achieve their dream of a free Scotland.

William Wallace was not the first who wanted to overthrow the British. Before Wallace took up the fight, there had been many men and women who died trying to defeat the British, but their efforts failed because, unlike Wallace, they were fighting for things they didn't believe in, such as more land or money for the nobles. Wallace came in with a truly defined purpose that united the people in a way they had never been before. By leading with his *why*, he gripped the hearts of the people and shared what he believed passionately, fervently, and articulately. He inspired a united uprising that led to a free Scotland.

SECOND STEP: BE AUTHENTIC

If you want people to listen to your story and be inspired by it, then you must ask yourself: Are my actions aligning with my words? If you have spent the time developing your story and are now sharing it with others, then it should represent your authentic story and not a story you *wish* was yours. The first step to freedom is honest answers to the five *W*'s. Be careful you don't answer with what you think the right answer *should* be; answer exactly what *is* in your current state. Do this and you'll achieve the results you're looking for.

As the old saying goes, "If it walks like a duck and it talks like a duck, it must be a duck." Authentic messaging will bring about authentic results. Sometimes people or businesses share a story, and you can tell in your gut the story is inauthentic. This isn't necessarily done on purpose, but it does keep that person or business from being free. Proactively ensure that wherever someone engages with your story, it matches exactly who you are. Perception leads to expectation. How you present yourself is what makes your first impression.

Take our politicians today as an example of this. How many times have we heard the right thing come out of new politicians' mouths, so they seem great on first impression, only to find their promises never get fulfilled? Or how many times have you gone into a new restaurant that had great advertisements, but when you sat down, the service was horrible or the food was bad? This happens time and time again. People don't like an inauthentic message. If you don't deliver on your promises, they will feel they've been tricked and will tune out.

Always tell the truth, no matter what, to ensure that when people engage with your message and engage with you, both their expectations and their experience are aligned. As a business owner, I get a lot of résumés sent to me from people looking for employment. After looking over their résumé (essentially their story) and then meeting them in person, I find either their résumé does or does not align with reality. In both instances the résumé creates a first impression. However, in the first instance, they establish trust because I find their message is authentic after meeting them in person. But in the second, the two don't align, and I do not give them a second interview.

PRACTICE! PRACTICE! PRACTICE!

You *can* get the results you desire by conveying an authentic story. To avoid missing expectations that you set from your story, know and articulate your message over and over again. Make sure to practice sharing your story consistently and with passion. We are conditioned to always answer with our *what*, because we're trained to ask what people do when we first meet them, even though we really just want to know if we like the person we're meeting. Instead of answering with what you do, tell them what you believe. Tell them your story. Then next time you're asked what you do, you can reply without hesitation and reap the benefits of your five *W*'s that much sooner.

If you have developed your story correctly and answered with your *why,* then they will remember you, even if they don't remember exactly what you do. It will be tough at first to share your story instead of answering with what you do, but in time and with practice, it will become second nature. Since people connect with the *why,* your story is the most important thing you can tell someone. As Jon Thomas wrote, your cause will "sit deep in their hearts."

It takes practice and hard work to think your story through, but the fruit of the labor is worth the effort. This book was written for the individual as well as the business audience, because to me they are one and the same. Being successful is about people, about building lasting and deep relationships. I want everyone reading this book to experience the freedom that comes with a well-developed story. While you may not be able to avoid every hit, you will be able to get back up faster, stronger, and ready to fight, so that in the end you can exclaim with pride, "Victory!"

LESSONS FROM THE RING

Before starting 4th Avenue Media, I was a TV reporter. As much fun as I had telling different stories each day, at first it wasn't easy doing it on live TV. Looking natural on camera takes a lot of practice. You're speaking at an inanimate object that gives you no feedback. Looking natural while telling a story is more than just art; it's hard work. Each day I got into the newsroom before my shift. I would watch and listen to myself report the news from the night before to observe my mannerisms and vocal inflections. I was looking for ways I could improve on how I delivered the stories I reported on.

After watching and listening to myself, I'd make the change that day.

For instance, when I first started I didn't know what to do with my hands when I was reporting. This is a common issue people face when they're in front of the camera. The overdone and unnatural tendency is to put the index finger and thumb of each hand together, making a sort of triangle, and that is exactly what I did my first few days. But I realized I never see people talking to each other with their hands like that off camera. Doing it was unnatural and inauthentic. So I corrected where my hands went, and the outcome was a more pleasant delivery of the story.

Once I was aware of how I delivered the stories, I practiced every day at getting better on my delivery. I got better, and so did my career. I encourage you to do the same thing with your story. Write out your story, and say it out loud over and over again. And I would even go as far as watching yourself in the mirror while delivering your story, until it flows out of you naturally and with passion.

2

REVVING THE ENGINE

W_____ ART THOU?

Answering the five questions of your story can be tough. Feel the pressure yet? Don't. Take a deep breath, relax, and think about your dream, whatever it is. In light of achieving your dream, what answers exist for you in the future? *What* were you born to do? In contrast to the future, what are the answers to each question in your present state? *Who* are you? *What* are you? *Where* are you? *When* are you? *Why* are you? Answering each question in future tense as well as present tense leads to an entirely different piece of your story, but put together, they are a powerful force, because they will show you who you actually are. Together they are your true story.

So let's begin with answering the question *who*. The answer to *who* is all about your character traits. What character traits are you comprised of right now? Are you a person of integrity? Are you loyal, hardworking, and motivated? Are you someone who loves to be part of a team, compassionate, quiet and observant? Whatever character traits you have, write them down as the answer to your *who*. All these individual words may not end up in your story when you deliver it to people you talk to, but you will be confident when you introduce yourself to someone. Your confidence will come from knowing that the person you are standing before others is fully aware of your character traits inwardly as well as outwardly.

What do you do? *What* do you want to be? *What* are you all about? Answering the *what* gets down to the tactical actions in your daily life. Usually we blanket the answers under our career or occupation. Sometimes *what* is defined by a hobby, such as music, art, or sports. Regardless of the answer, how you view your *what* in both the present and the future will determine what your future looks like. Inevitably when you think about your dream, your thoughts are of *what* you are doing. Take the time again to answer the *what* in both future and present state. Do this and you're on your way to a powerful story.

What about *how*, you ask? That is a great question and one I sometimes get when talking about the basics of a story. *How* is certainly an important question to answer, but *how* falls under your *what*. Without defining first your *what*, your *how* is irrelevant. If you are a planner, then answering the *how* may be important to you, but it is secondary to first developing your story and igniting your passion.

When answering *when*, I first start off with age. What year were you born? What decade do you associate yourself growing up in? *When* would you like to achieve your dream? *When* was the last time you tried to achieve your dream? Your *when* should hopefully be the easiest question to answer.

Location. Location. Location. It all comes down to location. Ever heard the sayings, "in the right place at the right time," or "wrong place at the wrong time"? *Where* you are is important. Ask not only *where* you're from, but also, *where* are you going? What does *where* look like now, and what will it look like when you reach your dream?

I've already defined what *why* is, but it's worth another look. As a consulting practice, it's important to ask someone *why* five times in order to get down to the real answer. Asking *why* reveals your passion. Answering *why* defines your belief. *Why* is a double-edged sword that makes people take notice when used properly.

SEPARATING THE BOYS FROM THE MEN

Even though *why* is the most important question to answer, if you don't have answers to the other questions, you'll still be left with an inauthentic message. As a 26-year-old entrepreneur starting a company, I was ambitious, inexperienced, and focused on one thing: building a large company. Unfortunately, my good intentions didn't always translate into good team-building or management. I knew my *why*, but I struggled with answering the other questions like *who* and *what*. Without writing down the answers, I was just working off wrong assumptions about my own ability carrying me through to the finish line.

I want to help people achieve their very best. I love inspiring a group of people to put forth maximum output in order to reap the maximum reward. In order to reap your maximum reward—which in this case is your dream—and apply your passion, you must know your whole story and then go forth and act on it. Unfortunately for me, like most of us, I had to learn the hard way.

LESSON LEARNED

I bootstrapped my company. I'd sell to grow, so I wouldn't be in debt to anyone. This worked well for all intents and purposes, but during the first year of the business, I ran into some rough times. Besides always worrying about having enough money in the bank to pay the bills and make payroll, I hired employees who turned out to be the wrong people to have on the team because I didn't know my *who* in the context of 4th Avenue Media's story.

I hired employees who were inexperienced in working in a professional culture. For most of them, working at 4th Avenue Media was their first job. Because I didn't define my *who*, somewhere in year two of the company, the tone changed. Disrespect and bad attitudes spread and became so caustic even my clients could tell something was going on.

Since it was the first "real" job for many of the employees, and I was new at managing people and busy building the company, I excused their bad attitudes. I was trying to create a laidback culture, because I didn't want to micromanage, but I got taken advantage of.

Before starting 4th Avenue Media, I had experienced the worst of the worst when it came to bosses or direct management, and I didn't want to create anything like what I went through. I tried to build processes and implement more structure in the business, but quickly realized that making sure everyone was on the same page was difficult. There were a lot of negative attitudes in the office those first few years.

The negativity came from either the employees or, at times, from me when I let the highs and lows of running a business show in my actions. Eventually, animosities grew within the company, and one by one the employees either quit or were fired. By the end of year two, I was the only person left in the office.

Shaken up after this experience, I kept wondering, "How could everything fall apart so quickly?" Something was wrong; I just didn't know what, but I did know it started with me. I thought I had a plan to fulfill my dream of building a successful agency, but I got knocked down, hard, because my story wasn't fully developed. I had not answered my *who*.

This happens all the time with people. We take a hit in our personal or professional lives, and it can seem impossible to get back up and start again. Looking back, I know now that the reason I was the only one left was because I didn't take time to answer what character traits defined my *who* at the beginning. I built my business on shaky ground, and it had to be rebuilt. The purpose of this story is to show you that it is possible to know very well your *why*, but ignore the *who*, and the result is an unfulfilled dream. Thankfully, it's never too late to develop the whole story and get on the path to freedom.

THE WHOLE STORY AND NOTHING BUT THE STORY

It took some time to answer the *who*. I wanted to make sure I had the right people in both skill set and attitude, but I was nervous to make the same mistakes again. I started reading books on hiring and building culture. The book that made the biggest difference was *The No Asshole Rule* by Dr. Robert Sutton, a Stanford University professor who wrote about successful companies who literally had this rule as part of their company culture. I highly recommend reading this book. It fascinated and inspired me and changed my perspective on team-building. I was tired of dealing with attitudes and people trying to move in directions other than the goal of the company. Eventually I asked myself what I was looking for in culture and how that culture fit within the story. Essentially, "What is my *who*, and how does it fit within my story?"

MAKING A U-TURN

Creating an about-face from the negativity, I put down on paper what was important to me in the culture of my business. Number one was serving the client in a positive environment, where gossiping, backstabbing, attitudes, and behavioral problems didn't exist. I put in writing rules that before I had thought were implied, such as no discussing employees' pay, lying to management, being late without prior notice, missing deadlines, or using offensive language in the workplace.

In business, in order to create and build a culture that engages people inside and out of the company in a positive way, you must answer your *who*. In your personal life make sure to surround yourself with the right people. You must know your *who*.

After reading Dr. Sutton's book, I implemented a code of conduct in my company to answer the *who*. The acronym for the code of conduct became DSAT, which stands for *Do right, Say right, Act right*, and *Think right*. The *who* of my company is always going to be good people who follow the Golden Rule—"Do unto others as you would have them do unto you"—both for each other and for clients at all times!

Every person I hired after implementing DSAT fit into my *who* as a company. We talked about DSAT every week at our team meetings and listened to each other explain what DSAT meant to them. The change was amazing. The culture inside the office was buzzing, and the work we produced drove amazing results for our clients. Another benefit of answering the *who* was that the relationship with my clients improved drastically. I could now focus on serving them better, instead of babysitting bad attitudes in the office and constantly trying to motivate people rowing in different directions.

Telling this story is important because I knew my *why*, *what*, *where*, and *when*, but it was the *who* that was missing. And I paid the price. *Who* you are is just as important as *why* you do what you do!

Although it was a struggle to define the story, once it was defined and everyone was rowing in the same direction, going to work became fun again. Working around a group of like-minded and focused individuals ignited each other's passion, and our work showed it.

3

YOU NEVER REALLY KNOW A MAN UNTIL YOU STAND IN HIS SHOES

DON'T BE COMPLACENT

Change is hard, but change is good. Winston Churchill said, "To improve is to change; to be perfect is to change often." This may be true, but changing is easier said than done. There's only one group of humans in history who like change: babies with dirty diapers. The rest of us have a hard time with it. The reason most people resist change is because it requires effort to learn something new, admit we're wrong, or cause an about-face in our viewpoint. If we're honest with ourselves, we'll acknowledge we've never done anything we didn't want to do. So when circumstance demands we change, we have to admit that what we want to do isn't working and adapt.

But like any great story, change takes us on a journey of the unknown, and it can seem daunting. For business owners this can be especially difficult if they've been in business for any real length of time. The status quo becomes comfortable, and doing something different to get the same desired outcome as they've had for years seems unnecessary. But for anyone who has a dream and doesn't see it being realized, it's time to admit change is necessary.

As the old saying goes, "The world is changing, and so must we." The speed at which we can find information about anything we want on the Internet is staggering. Computers and mobile devices have transformed the world as we know it. Libraries used to be one of the only places to get information. Now you can get information about everything and anything with a click of a button. Messages that used to take days to send through the mail can now be sent instantly. Cellphones began as devices that only allowed direct calls from one phone to another, and now cellphones are mini-computers, storing your life's information in the palm of your hand. As our environment has changed due to factors like technology, the question is, are we adapting with the change?

TEST YOUR STORY

In 2008, I had a dream for a business that didn't fit neatly into a category of marketing: tell the story of a business by producing TV-style news stories for companies, and post the video on their website. The idea took off from the start. Thanks to the growing use of YouTube, online video was no longer just goofy videos, but engaging, professionally produced content—and I can confidently say that we were one of the best at producing it.

As I was focused on producing videos to post online, business owners started asking if 4th Avenue Media offered other services, such as website design, social media management, or other marketing services. There was an obvious need to be filled, but it required me to rethink my business. I hired graphic designers, branding specialists, and social media experts to answer the need. Surrounding myself with a team where each employee had their own category of expertise, I was able to answer *yes* when before I had answered *no*. Because I changed and adapted, my company grew and so did the relationships I had with my clients.

Adapting allowed my company to triple our revenue within one year. The change I made was easy, because the principle of storytelling applied to all services we offered. Without adapting, I wouldn't have been able to grow my company and would have gone out of business.

GROWING PAINS

Have you ever met someone who is determined to force their will to happen, when it's obvious what they're trying to do isn't working? For entrepreneurs this happens all too often, and unfortunately the results usually end up hurting them financially and emotionally.

No matter how much you *want* your idea to come to fruition, an idea is just that, an idea. What makes the difference is execution. You never know if an idea to fulfill your dream will work until you try, right? When you try something out, you figure out pretty quickly if it works or not. But it can be hard to see the forest among the trees. If you have an idea for what your dream looks like but don't see things working smoothly right away, adapt and grow with the opportunity that change can bring—that is, with the assumption you are working within the confines of your authentic story.

Adaptation is defined as *an effective change in response to an altered situation.* Adapting is important in order for you to benefit in the long run. Getting hit in the face makes you rethink everything you're doing. Why am I here doing this? What's the benefit? When will I see the light at the end of the tunnel? Figuring out the answers and adapting is crucial to keeping yourself going toward your dream even when you get hit. It's crucial to Victory.

Think, what is that wall in your life you just can't seem to get past? Is it negatively impacting your morale or production inside company walls? By adapting to current circumstances, you can effectively navigate through or around that wall.

Perhaps you have a great idea, and maybe it actually works but not at the level of success you're hoping for. If you have an idea and it's not working the way you want, make the necessary changes. Maybe you need to keep your idea on the back burner and watch for the perfect time to reintroduce your idea to the marketplace.

Always watch. Always listen. Don't fall asleep on the job. Your dream is in sight.

FOOL'S GOLD

When you're busy adapting to new circumstances, it can be easy to lose sight of your story. Regardless of opportunity, if what you are trying to accomplish doesn't line up with your story, then either rethink your story from the foundation up, or ignore opportunities that don't align with who you are. Build your authentic story, because the inauthentic story is like fool's gold. It may look good at first, but in reality it is worthless.

No one likes a poser, a fake, a phony. These types of people cannot be trusted, and the same applies to an inauthentic story. Often a person or company claims one thing when the reality is completely different. This leads to a lack of trust and eventually isolation. Don't forget what you believe. Don't lose why you have a dream in the first place.

BE A BROADCASTER

So what if you *are* communicating your authentic story but still not seeing the desired results? The problem may be *how* you are communicating your story. No matter how passionate you are about communicating your message, without keeping the audience in mind, you let it fall on deaf ears. An impactful message is not what's conveyed, but what is received. Even if you come up with your own carefully crafted language, it means nothing if it doesn't resonate with your audience.

I frequently encounter business owners who fail to think of their audience. When describing their business, they share a lot of facts and figures. They begin the conversation with their *what*. Because they are so focused on the *what*, they miss out on an opportunity to tailor the message to their audience. Consequently, they end up sounding just like their competition.

For example, think about going to the grocery store and looking at all the products on the shelf. Let's say a common product you buy is laundry detergent. You look on the shelf, and there are multiple different brands that essentially all do the same thing: clean your clothes. The one you choose sticks out because they tell a story. They don't lead with their *what*; they lead with their *why*. Between competition within the same product or service category, the *what* will look similar across the board. Developing your unique story and leading with your *why* is the most powerful way to make you stand out to your audience.

I don't want you to think, though, that by changing how you convey your message you are in some way being fake or insincere. In our laundry detergent example, the brand could probably talk all day about its chemical components and the science behind its cleaning power. But you, as the consumer, most likely don't understand (or care) about any of that. So instead, the brands develop messaging that resonates with you. Do you feel lied to when detergent companies lead their branding with its lavender scent and not science? Didn't think so. The way you deliver your story is also meeting a need, and it's just as important as the message itself.

Are you adapting to your audience when you convey your story? Are you being authentic when you convey your story? Answering these two questions will dramatically help you, as you'll easily be able to adapt and navigate through the myriad of changes that are constantly coming at you and your audience.

4

TIP OF THE SPEAR

DRAWING BLOOD

In battle when men used swords and engaged in hand-to-hand combat, preparation was made prior to the fight in order to sharpen their weapons and ensure that the blade in their hands was as effective as it possibly could be. The sharper the end of the sword or the spear, the easier it was to achieve victory. One of my rules for success is that a person or business must first know what their *tip of the spear* is and then ensure it is as sharp as possible, so they can charge into the field of battle and win. It's about victory. It's about passion. And it's about your story.

In the world of storytelling, there are really two ways to tell a story. The two types of stories that people tune in for and engage with are called the Inverted Pyramid and Pyramid models. You've seen or heard both of these models used in traditional media.

The Inverted Pyramid model is used most often in newspapers and top stories on TV news. You start with the broad lead and work your way down to describe the details. For instance, *a 56-year-old Seattle man died in a car accident on I-5. Witnesses say he swerved into oncoming traffic. Police assessed the speed at which he was traveling at around 50 miles per hour. No one else was injured. He is survived by his wife and two children. A memorial will be held this Saturday.*

That's a great and to-the-point way to tell a story. It does answer the five *W*'s, and when we're in a hurry, that's the best way for us to consume the facts and move on with our day. However, if your goal is to connect with people on an emotional level, it is not the most effective method. People are looking for a connection, and it is for that reason that newspaper readership has declined. Newspapers are full of Inverted Pyramid stories, but they contain very little emotion.

One of my good friends wrote for *The Seattle Times* and now writes for ESPN. I told him in 2008 that *The Seattle Times* should have each reporter voice their story and have the audio version of the newspaper available online with a link to the audio on the printed newspaper itself. If they ended up doing that, people could emotionally connect more with Inverted Pyramid-style stories by connecting with the voice of the writer.

My friend said that no one in management would ever go for it because a reporter isn't supposed to have a personality that people connect with. The stories they write should just be about the content and nothing more. The writers with a personality are the columnists, not the general-assignment reporters. As we've seen, newspapers didn't adapt and little to no emotion was produced in their product, the audience shrunk and many went out of business. Dream over.

Newspapers should have realized that people don't want every writer to be a columnist but that most readers would enjoy hearing the voice of the writer, because most people connect with the emotional aspect of a story over facts or figures. Unfortunately, the newspaper industry missed the mark, but you don't have to.

The best way to emotionally connect with an audience is the Pyramid model, where you lead with your *why*. In storytelling I call this the *tip of the spear* because it is the first thing a person comes in contact with. Just as a sharp spear would surely make an impact (literally) on the battlefield, so does a well-crafted story with an audience. Whether you're giving your elevator pitch to a networking group, talking about your company in a sales meeting, or coming up with a marketing plan, delivering a Pyramid story will connect with your audience and build rapport, establishing credibility more quickly. That's how all episodic TV shows are written: "Tune in next week to find out more." It takes you on a journey and connects with your curiosity.

Maybe while watching TV you've heard a story like this:

On a sunny Saturday morning in March, George Jones mows the lawn. He wakes up early to get started and makes sure each blade is perfectly manicured. He follows the same routine every Saturday for years. One day, he finds out his lawnmower was stolen. He looks and looks but to no avail. His passion for mowing the lawn seems at an end. Then one night he gets a knock on his door, only to find a brand-new mower with a card on it. "Dear Mr. Jones, you've inspired me to work harder at work, and because of that I got a raise. I took your old mower and bought this new mower for you, so you can inspire more people each week." Mr. Jones starts mowing the lawn again and inspires the entire community to make their own lawns look good and keep up with the man who for years has dedicated his Saturdays to mowing.

This type of story takes you on a journey. A good story is like a river. A river goes fast, then slows down and bends to the left, then to the right, always keeping you on your toes as you engage with it. You may know the destination, but the experience to get there is what makes the journey exciting and worth coming back for.

When you share your story, what type of story are you sharing? Are you hitting your audience with a Pyramid or Inverted Pyramid story model? If you want to connect with the heart of your audience then always share your Pyramid model story.

A CALL TO ACTION

Another thing my dad always told me growing up is, people are waiting to be told what to do. The media knows this, and it's why they always direct their audience to make an action. They'll say, *Don't go away*, *Stay tuned*, or *Watch tonight at five*. If you want your audience to take action, give them a call to action after you share your story.

The TV show *60 Minutes* employs some of the best storytellers in the industry. Each story they tell is in the Pyramid style, so you keep watching. *60 Minutes*, like most TV news shows, also "teases down" future stories so you continue to watch. You should be doing the same thing when you tell a story or want to promote it. Tell people to tune in at another time for more information or meet with you for coffee after they hear your story to find out more. The right audience will act, and you'll reap the benefit.

HAVING THE RIGHT PLAN

The Pyramid model works great when engaging with your audience, but there is a place and time for an Inverted Pyramid model—for example, business plans. Business plans are important, and so is knowing how to write one. As I entered my fifth year of business at 4th Avenue Media, I had an Inverted Pyramid plan, which kept me focused and acted as the road sign along the journey, pointing in the right direction. It took me a while to figure out that an Inverted Pyramid-style business plan is the best way to go, but once I did, I had clarity to achieve my company's vision. I started with my lead and worked down into the details. How you are going about developing your story in life or in business affects where it takes you.

I learned the hard way that everyone has a plan until they get punched in the face. I started 4th Avenue Media based off the Pyramid model, figuring out the details along the way. I blindly navigated through murky waters, trying whatever would work—and I was getting punched daily. I didn't have a business background. I was fresh from the newsroom, where making deadlines and connecting with people was my number-one priority. At the time, writing a business plan was like learning a foreign language. But I can tell you now that if you are going to start a business, save yourself the headaches and write an Inverted Pyramid business plan.

Dave Samuels of Demand Media states that creating a business plan allows you to identify potential problems and opportunities your business might face; avoid penalties, fines, or other legal problems; adapt to changes in the marketplace; and expand or contract from a position of objectivity. You can share a business plan with potential partners, advisers, and sources of funding. The Small Business Administration suggests that a business plan be a work in progress that you should keep current. It's an inverted story meant to provide clarity.

THE OVERVIEW EFFECT

Amidst all the hits and punches life will throw your way, how will you avoid the burnout and stay positive and motivated throughout the journey? The best thing you can do for yourself is to think of the outcome and stay focused. Remind yourself often what your dream looks like, and keep going toward it.

I have a saying I tell my employees: "Don't tell me what you can't do. Tell me what you *can* do, and do it." This world is a hard and nasty place at times, and it can sometimes seem that everyone is telling you that you can't make it, or won't make it. This kind of negative influence can drive our internal voice to agree with those people. It breeds self-doubt, creating thoughts of "I can't do that," instead of "I'll try" or "I can, and I will." Unless you have a direct line to God and he told you that you can't, all that noise is just conjecture. What matters is what you want to get out of your life or your business. What is your dream?

As I said in Chapter 1, write out your story. Put it down on paper so you can clearly see the answers. Answer the *who, what, when, where,* and *why*. Ponder the questions and keep asking the questions until you strip down the answer to the unvarnished truth. Don't rush through this process. It's crucial to take your time, develop your story, and stay on track in your journey. Whether it takes a day, a week, or a month, stick with it until it becomes glaringly obvious to you.

Writing out your story will give you perspective on why you do the things you do and allow you to see if there's meaning in it or not. As I've mentioned before, money isn't why you do something. Your *why* may be what money can do for you, but it's not money alone. Thinking of your outcome, figuring out your *why*, and staying focused will enable you to achieve success.

The issue really becomes focusing on the end versus focusing on the means. If you focus on your end, then no matter how many times you get punched, blocked, or rejected, you'll have the wherewithal to get back up and keep trying. This is why the second habit in Stephen Covey's book *The 7 Habits of Highly Effective People* is "begin with the end in mind." If you are constantly focusing on the means, and how you feel changes with your circumstances, then I guarantee you'll quit pursuing your dream and get swept downstream. Stay in the fight. Hit back when you need to, and strive to win. You can do it. You will do it!

CHAPTER 5

IT'S NOT YOUR
MAMA'S FAIRYTALE

ADORING FANS

No matter where you go, who you are, or what you do, you have an audience—a group of people who engage with you and your content. If you have customers, you have an audience. If you work a job, you have an audience. If you have friends, you have an audience. For a business, it's the people who follow and are interested in your brand.

The beautiful thing about having an audience is that they can keep you motivated. In the journey toward achieving your dream, sometimes passion can fade when the road seems long. When you have people around you who believe the same thing as you, you can lean on them in order stay inspired when times get tough. Having an audience that shares your belief not only helps keep you motivated, but it will inevitably lead them to share your story with others who believe the same thing. This is called *word-of-mouth*.

Most marketing experts agree that word-of-mouth marketing is the most powerful way to grow your audience, and for the most part, they are right. Even if you have an amazing story, when it comes down to it, people listen to others they trust. Gaining an audience of loyal, adoring fans who share information about you to their friends is invaluable to your credibility and success. Share your story, and share it boldly!

A great example of an organization that shares stories is traditional media, especially TV stations. The goal of any station is to make their general audience become loyal, consistent viewers (adoring fans) of specific content. They count on an audience growing when people share shows they like with their friends. We've all flipped through the channels and seen a promo on TV, or we've heard the radio promoting content. And then we asked our friends to watch it with us. Since our friends have common beliefs, word-of-mouth ensured the right people tuned in to the message. Then they asked their friends to watch, thus continuing the cycle of others tuning in. The result is passionate fans engaging with a passionate story.

In the television industry, there are hundreds of pilot episodes produced every year, but some never even see the light of day. Even if a show makes it to "Prime Time," it may still be cancelled. If this happens, it's because the show's story doesn't resonate with the right audience. Since it doesn't resonate, no one cares enough to tell others to tune in. Hence the show eventually gets cancelled, and no one cares and eventually no one remembers. The same goes for the person who doesn't share their story with passion to others who believe the same thing. If you don't have an audience for your story, your dream will be essentially cancelled and eventually forgotten.

THE SIX-PACK

If you have a happy, satisfied audience and adoring fans, then you are adequately answering the five *W*'s. But more than likely, you are also answering the sixth and final question to a great story, and that is, *so what?* By answering *so what*, you are telling others why they should care and how they can benefit from your story. At the end of the day, people are only going to love and share your story with others when they see the benefit for themselves. Answering *so what* puts yourself in your audience's shoes and says why they should care. The *so what* is what you look for when hearing someone's story, so ensuring you answer *so what* in your own story is living out the Golden Rule. As you would want someone to tell you a story in context of how you could benefit from it, you should do the same.

Every individual and every business in the world would benefit by joining what I call the Golden Rule Revolution. The Golden Rule: treat others as you would like to be treated. Revolution: a sudden, extreme, or complete change in the way people live and work. We all may know the Golden Rule in our minds, but it's time to see the Golden Rule in our actions. It seems simple enough, but in reality it can be hard to do, but not impossible!

I learned early on in my career the importance of *so what*. My very first reporting job was in a small market where I reported live every morning. About a year into my job, I was able to travel to Spokane, Washington, for a conference and sit down with journalist legend Al Tompkins of the Poynter Institute. After looking at my demo tape, he told me something I'll never forget: "You keep answering *what* in your story, but I never hear you answer the most important question, *so what*. I can't tell you how many times I've seen reporters reporting that a building's on a fire, while we can clearly see the fire by the flames shooting out behind their head," he said. "They fail to answer a crucial question for the audience: *So What*?!" For instance, it's not just that the apartment was on fire, but you, as the audience, should always make sure to turn off your appliances before going on vacation. You listen and benefit from the *so what* in the story.

When Tompkins told me that, it completely changed the way I saw storytelling and how I wrote and delivered my stories. I began to start with the audience in mind. I realized I wasn't answering the five *W*'s for my own benefit, but for the people who tuned in to my content, who found benefit from watching. The audience became priority number one, and I always made sure to answer that crucial sixth question.

The *so what* portion of your story will make the most meaningful connection with your audience out of all the questions you can answer, because deep down, that's what people really care about. Developing your story with *who, what, when, where,* and *why* helps you stay on your feet and keep going when life gives you a black eye (or two). The difference in answering *so what* in addition to the other five questions is that it enables you to *hit back* and continue to pursue your dream.

I FEEL YOUR PAIN

When you tell your story and live by the Golden Rule by answering *so what,* you are applying empathy. Living by the Golden Rule takes empathy—being able to understand and act on your audience's values and point of view. When distributing your story, empathy should be behind everything you do. Like Bill Clinton once famously said, "I feel your pain," and his audience loved him for it.

As the saying goes, "People don't care how much you know until they know how much you care." Empathy is the key to building your audience. Tony Smith, Superintendent of Oakland Unified School District, said in an interview: "We have to be able to understand our own experiences emotionally to have a better relationship with others in the world and also to engage deeply in dialogue, to take other people's perspective and examine our own." When you take the time to understand your own experiences and the experiences of your audience, you can act on the Golden Rule and build trust, loyalty, and the right audience. Because you are answering the *so what*, people will feel understood and will be more likely to listen, remember, and share your story.

6

WAX ON... WAX OFF...
WAX ON... WAX OFF

BEING MR. MIYAGI

Whoever you are and wherever you're at along the journey of story development and distribution, it's time you became like Mr. Miyagi. The fictional karate master from the movie *The Karate Kid* has a lot to teach us about expertise. When Mr. Miyagi singlehandedly defeated five attackers using karate, he instantly established himself as an expert in the subject to his pupil, Daniel. When Daniel then became his student, Mr. Miyagi gave the instructions, and Daniel followed them.

The Mr. Miyagi story is an example of a philosophy I have called the 10/90 Rule. In the 10/90 Rule, 10 percent of the world population is hypothetically doctors. The 90 goes to the 10 and tells the 10 what's wrong. The 10 writes a prescription on a piece of paper and gives it to the 90, and the 90 will swallow whatever was prescribed. The 90 never thinks twice about the pill they swallowed, where it's manufactured, or why it's colored the way it is. The 10 told the 90 to do it, and so the 90 does it. We all rely on experts, the 10s, to give us advice and tell us what to do, whether in medicine or otherwise. Similarly, people are relying on you to be the expert on your own story.

As a test of my philosophy, I told my wife's cousin, who was in residency at the time, about the 10/90 Rule. When I told him about the Rule, he laughed at the truth of it. He told me that when he first started out, he didn't know every condition people were dealing with. If he had a question or wasn't sure about a condition, he would excuse himself, walk out of the room, and immediately start flipping through a medical book to find the answer. When he walked back into the room, he was calm, cool, and collected. He never broke stride when looking his patients in the eye and recommending the remedy. He was the 10.

Everyone must strive to be the 10 in their respective area of expertise. Most business owners are 10 percent in their field, but the smart owners surround themselves with other 10s to accommodate for each strength and minimize weakness.

When you are a 10, people trust you, but trust isn't something given or gained easily. When we trust our doctors to mend a broken bone, trust our plumber to fix our leaky faucet, or trust an airplane pilot to fly us to our favorite vacation spot, we know they are experts in their field. However, we also know they have put in a lot of work to become that expert, thus fostering trust. If you have put in the work to become an expert (a 10), then people will treat you as such. Perpetuating a healthy 10/90 relationship with others is absolutely necessary in achieving your dream.

In Malcom Gladwell's bestseller *Outliers*, he states that it takes 10,000 hours (or about 5 years) of "deliberate practice" to become an expert. Instead of being a jack-of-all-trades, it's better to figure out what you can specialize in and leave the rest to others. As the old proverb says, "Plow deep before plowing wide."

If it really does take 10,000 hours to become an expert, then you must be selective in what you put your time and effort into. That's why pursuing your dream with passion and surrounding yourself with people who can help you achieve that dream is crucial. One thing to watch out for is articulating your story as though you are the expert, when you are still in the process of becoming the 10.

We all have our areas of strength, and together with others that have complementary strengths, we make an effective team. Always defer answers to those who have the expert answers rather than trying to fake it. You can find the right answer, but you don't necessarily have to know off the top of your head. Over time you'll eventually become a 10, and your relationships will be stronger because of it.

As a young entrepreneur, I was eager to make a sale for

my company, and at times it required me to "fake it until I make it" for the sale. I communicated a story that made me sound like the expert when in fact I had not become one yet in every service I sold. What I quickly learned was, since I couldn't deliver as the expert in every area I'd pitch a sale for, I didn't fulfill upon the promise in my story and lost trust with the client. To no surprise, those business relationships didn't last. In order to solve this issue, I sought knowledge to become the expert or hired those who were. This way I could fulfill upon my promise as the 10 in my story.

KEEPING THE RATIO

When I work with a client and they respect me as the 10, the relationship goes smoothly, and the client is happy with what I produce. I deliver great value, and the results exceed expectations. But when the client tries to do or influence part of my work, they leave their 10 and creep into my 10. This creeping causes the working relation-ship to break down.

When a relationship moves out of the 10/90 ratio, the work is good and the business relationship is okay, but neither of us is working as the expert. My job is to serve the client's needs, but sometimes what the client *needs* and what the client *wants* are two totally different things. When we stay in the 10, we can articulate our points in an authoritative way, and our audience will listen. But when we fall out of the 10, it's more difficult to get the results both parties seek.

The worst relationship of all is when you find yourself in a situation where the client second-guesses everything you do, is never happy with what is produced, and will probably be looking for your replacement shortly after starting to work with you.

How does this relate to you and your story? Make sure that the people you surround yourself with respect you and your story for the value that it provides. If we are on the wrong team, then our desired results from our story will not be realized. If we don't trust those we surround ourselves with, then we need to make a change.

We need to strive to become experts in our story, and when we do become the 10, we need to work with others who trust us to be the 10 and understand their working relationship as our audience is in the 90 category. The same can be said for us when we are listening to someone who knows their authentic story. In that situation we are the 90, and they are the 10. Our job as part of the team is to help each other win.

ANOTHER LESSON FROM THE RING

Just as you need to be selective in what you specialize in, you should also be selective in what clients you choose to work with, or business you work for. Working with or for anyone who doesn't treat you with respect is a recipe for disaster. As an employee, how many times have we hated how we've been treated? The same can be true with a client. I have had some extremely rude people hire my firm. In the end, they may have gotten what they wanted, but the cost to my company and our morale was not worth the money.

I had a client that constantly tried to talk me down in price, and then once I agreed and did the work, he would complain that the work wasn't what he wanted, even though what we delivered was exactly what we agreed upon. This happened over and over again, until I finally fired the client by telling him we would no longer be taking more work from him. He was shocked and said some nasty things to me, but after he gave me a piece of his mind for being fired, not only was I free from constantly striving to please him, but my company and employees were free from constantly not feeling good enough and we could focus on the right relationships.

Since then, I've learned to work only with people I think will be a good fit for my agency. A well-fitting client will see you as the 10 and stay in the 90, and they will treat you with respect. Anything less than that is simply not worth it.

7

MIRROR, MIRROR, ON THE WALL, WHO IS THE MOST AUTHENTIC OF THEM ALL?

CULTURE AND LANGUAGE

When I lived in San Antonio, working as the feature reporter for a local affiliate, I hosted a nightly segment where I immersed myself in the local culture and told unique stories that resonated with the nightly audience. However, I had a problem: I couldn't roll my *R*'s. Since the population at that time was 60 percent Hispanic, this posed a problem.

One night after reporting on a bakery, which in Spanish is called a *panadaria*, I got on-air and pronounced the *R* without rolling it. As soon as I left the studio and got back to my desk, I got a phone call from a viewer who told me that if I were going to be on-air in San Antonio, I need to learn how to roll my *R*'s.

I told the viewer that I had tried for years to roll my *R*'s. I had even taken five years of Spanish classes. Even now, no matter what I try, rolling my *R*'s remains physically impossible for me.

I spent some time thinking about why that person who called me felt it was so important for me to roll my *R*'s. I came to understand that even though I was speaking the language, I wasn't speaking it properly, and therefore I wasn't fitting into the culture of my audience.

As a reporter I was supposed to be a part of the culture I was speaking to in order to be trusted as a credible news source. I know Spanish because I took five years of it, two in high school and three in college. But my inability to roll my *R*'s kept me from being 100 percent part of the culture in San Antonio. I will never be part of that culture perfectly, even if I move to Mexico City and live there the rest of my life. I could dress the part, know the terrain, love the people, and eat the food, but unless I learn how to roll my *R*'s, I'll remain an outsider.

This specific example brought to light that we have a much closer tie between language and culture than we often realize. What this showed me was that people engage with culture, and not language itself. Rolling my *R*'s was a *cultural* detail I was lacking. When I started thinking about this in business terms, I realized the same concept applies to how a story is told and how it conveys brand authenticity. This is important because your brand is everything that someone engages with. It's the feeling that your story gives, and it's the identity derived from your story.

Seth Godin explains brand this way: A brand is the set of expectations, memories, stories, and relationships that, taken together, account for a person's decision to choose one product or service over another. If the consumer (whether a business, a buyer, a voter, or a donor) doesn't pay a premium, make a selection, or spread the word, then no brand value exists for that consumer.

You must speak in a language that reflects your *culture,* because your brand is derived from your culture. Here is my premise: A language defines a culture, and every business has a culture. Therefore, every business must have a language. The same goes for the individual. You have a language and a culture that affects who your audience is and how they engage with you.

Before I came to this conclusion, the creative work my company developed for clients would sometimes miss the mark. This happened because we were creating the identity and brand based off of language and not culture. We would ask clients to tell us about themselves, and they would rattle off a list of words that all had to do with *what* they did or sold. We would design their branding based on the list of words they gave us. But those words didn't reflect their authentic culture—they only reflected the company's language.

Every person or business has a unique language: vernacular words that are spoken in the halls, offices, and lobbies; to clients, team members, and managers. It is this language that defines the culture. If you want to make sure your story is authentic to your brand, then you must write down your vernacular words and then do a word association from your language list. Write those words down as well, and that will give you your culture list. From your culture, pick the words that stand out to you, and you'll define your brand words.

Based on this logic, I created a process to derive the authentic brand of a company. I call it *The Mirror Test* because the brand that is developed as a result of this test accurately reflects the culture—thus, the mirror. It is a process where I first extract the *language* words of a company. I then use the language list to extract the *culture* words of a company, and lastly I use the culture list to extract the *brand* words of a company. This enables me to develop an authentic brand that their story must affirm.

You must base your story on your brand words so the experience people have of you is how you *want* them to experience you. When their actual experience and your ideal experience align, you have developed a perfectly authentic story.

BRAND

So, what happens when your brand is not authentic, when what you portray to the world doesn't align with what people experience in person? This next story from when I was a reporter in San Antonio is a good example:

San Antonio has a hugely popular festival called Fiesta, and the Grand Marshal of the Fiesta parade was a famous actor from a hit TV show in the 90s (whose name I am omitting on purpose). I granted the exclusive interview with him since my station was the sponsor of Fiesta.

The interview was to take place in the lobby of a hotel on the Riverwalk at 5 PM, with the story to go live at 9. However, the actor did not show up on time for his interview. As my camera operator and I, along with fans who wanted to meet the actor, waited for him, five turned to six, and six turned to seven—despite the fact that one of the actor's "people" kept promising he would be down any minute. It was 7 PM when I made the call to the station to let them know the actor hadn't come down yet and I wouldn't be able to turn the story. The producers in the newsroom were scrambling to figure out how to fill my five-minute segment if I didn't have a story, which was especially difficult since my story had been heavily promoted all day.

As we started packing up and began walking out of the lobby, we heard the actor was finally coming down the hall, so we set back up. He walked up to us, and instead of apologizing for his tardiness, he just said arrogantly, "Let's do this." But as soon as we turned the camera light on, all of a sudden the actor turned into this humble, quiet, and reserved person—the person he portrayed on-screen. The audience who came to watch the interview were fans of this actor, and they witnessed the blatant disconnect between the on-screen actor and the "actor" in real life.

The result of this nonalignment was immediately apparent. By the time I was done with the interview, not one person was left waiting to meet him besides hotel staff. Everyone saw the obvious change in demeanor and how inauthentic this actor was. The only time they had engaged with him prior was with the persona or brand that he had created and distributed to his audience. But when time came to engage with him in person, people saw how fraudulent he was, and it ruined his credibility to those standing there.

Having an authentic brand is crucial to longevity and creating brand advocates. It is crucial to creating people who will share your story because they know it's true. There is an article in *Entrepreneur* magazine that says, "Be true to your brand. Customers won't return to you— or refer you to someone else—if you don't deliver on your brand promise." That is exactly what I saw happen with this actor. He portrayed himself as humble, when in reality he was anything but. When people saw that difference they disengaged.

KEEP IT CONSISTENT

No matter how someone engages with your brand, it must be 100 percent consistent with the experience they have of you in person. Have you ever walked into a business after engaging with their advertising and find that the business itself didn't align with what it presented itself to be? This happens often and is a big reason why some businesses don't make it. Their brand is inconsistent with reality. Messaging and advertising create certain expectations, and when those expectations aren't met, people lose their trust in that brand. A business advisor told me once that "business is based on honesty." Relationships are also based on honesty, and it takes a relationship to create a customer for a business. So if your brand isn't honest, then you will not build lasting relationships with your audience.

If you don't deliver an authentic story, then you are equivalent to the person out fishing. Drop bait and wait, hoping to attract and catch a fish. But people are not fish. You can only catch a fish once, and you can only trick someone once. Fishing for your audience doesn't work. If you want to attract the right audience, then you must deliver authentic content around your story and build trust. It's that simple.

Instead of thinking of your audience as a fish on the other end of the line, think empathetically about your message and what you're sharing. Would you like to be treated like you are treating your audience? Would you buy from you based on your messaging or what you're selling? If the answer is *yes*, then keep it going. But if your answer is *no* and you are willing to make a change, then congratulations, you're on your way to an honest and successful transformation. The results you're looking for are in sight.

CHAPTER 8

CLOUDY WITH A CHANCE OF AWESOME

THERE'S MORE THAN ONE

I had been in business for two years when I began getting frustrated. I felt like I was doing great work for clients, but I had a hard time figuring out what the return on investment was for them. When asked, my clients' usual response was that they couldn't tell me or said it was hard to track. As time went on and the size of my client grew, so did my disappointment with their inability to track the benefit of my company telling their story.

One night in my office, while staring at a sign with our tagline—"The only thing that sets you apart is your story"—something clicked within my mind. It all made sense to me in a moment, and that night I restructured how I delivered my client's story.

What I realized that night was, it's not just your story that sets you apart, but your *stories* that set you apart. Once you define your authentic story, everything you do and say must be wrapped up in stories around your original brand story. It's your stories that people tune in for, and it's your stories that your audience wants to connect with. Your audience wants to continually engage with your brand. When you don't present the next story to tune in for, then people begin to tune out, and you lose the opportunity to build a stronger relationship. Without the right relationships, it's difficult to achieve your dream.

Accept that everyone has stories to tell. The question becomes, what stories do you want the world to know about you? What are the Pyramid-style stories that you can tell about the not-so-obvious things in your life that your audience would find fascinating? Spend time thinking that through so the stories you produce will return measurable results in helping you achieve your vision.

BECOMING A MEDIA CHANNEL

So you've got your stories. Now what? Now it's time to start acting like a media station. The media (a means of mass communication) is the most influential entity in the world. What the media says about any given topic is socially accepted on a wide scale. No matter the language, location, or demographic, the media reaches across all boundaries.

How does the media have so much power? The people in the media present themselves as the experts and produce content to an audience that is waiting to receive their stories. At a basic level, you are no different, but the game is changing. The broadcast, mass communication model worked well for television in particular and produced a lot of revenue for each station. A big reason it was so successful was because in the early years of broadcast TV, there weren't many players in the game. Your options were ABC, NBC, or CBS, or later, FOX.

Yet in the mid-'70s, premium cable began to rise in popularity. The content that was being produced became more specific to viewer preferences and interests and elicited a positive response. Cable basically said, "We don't care about the audience that's not interested in our programming; we care only about the people who *are* interested." With so many new stations popping up with unique content, we began to see specialty channels such as the Hunting Channel. This channel produced content only for those people who like hunting and who know more people who like hunting and can spread the word about the programming.

The cable TV model of selective content has become the norm of today's media consumer. Whether on-air, online, or in hand, people now expect to engage with the content they choose, and they have the power to ignore the rest. The broadcast model of distributing content is antiquated and ineffective.

Up until now, people have been acting like a broadcast model with a traditional mindset. This is especially true in business, where sharing a broad story that doesn't speak to a specific audience ends up costing a lot of money with little to no result. The time for that change is now.

Think of your attempts to reach your audience in terms of ammunition. It's expensive to waste a round, just like it's expensive to market you or your company in the broadcast mindset. By acting like a broadcast channel, you are using a shotgun approach, hoping to get a wider reach and hit a moving target. Cable is like using a rifle—one round per target, never wasting a shot.

DEFINING YOUR AUDIENCE

If you think of yourself as a cable channel instead of a broadcast channel, then understanding your audience becomes incredibly clear. It's not about quantity, but quality.

Birds of a feather flock together—meaning that one person who spends a thousand dollars with you will probably know others who will also spend a thousand dollars. Look at the trends and determine who your audience is right away. When you deliver specific content, more like-minded people will start tuning in to your content, and word will spread about the value you provide.

Once you define your audience and stop using the shotgun approach to communication, you can craft targeted stories that your audience will engage with. Over time, they will come to expect more of those stories from you and will tell others about you. While on the journey toward your dream, these people will be there to lean on and help you achieve the Victory you're looking for.

A valuable exercise to determine who you *think* your audience is versus who they actually are is to look at who is surrounding you *right now*. Who is attracted to your current message? Instead of thinking there are different groups of people out there who haven't heard your message yet, you should invest in those who have. Start by writing down the characteristics of the people currently surrounding you. For the business, write down the traits of your current customers. Find similarities or trends that may determine what they're attracted to in relation to your story.

Many companies make the mistake of assuming there are more, different types of people who will engage with their content. However, this is very unlikely. What's more likely is that there are more people who are similar to your *current* audience who just haven't heard about you yet. Sharing stories that are authentic to your brand story is how you enlarge your audience and build brand advocates.

STOP, COLLABORATE, AND LISTEN

As any good relationship goes, both parties' share, and both parties listen. Sharing your story in content, advertising, and social platforms allows people to receive your message. Listening to what they say back is just as important. You should encourage feedback to your story. Listening to your audience and adapting to their needs is how you develop deeper and stronger relationships that will drive the results you're looking for.

When sharing your story with your audience, it's important to keep in mind how they receive content. When it comes to a story, it's not the message conveyed, but the message received that makes the difference between a successful story and one that falls on deaf ears. If you're not speaking in a way your audience understands, you're wasting your breath. You have to deliver content with context, because content without context can be a very dangerous thing. To give context you must answer the *so what* of your story.

It's time to inspire. It's time to share. And it's time to listen to the feedback that comes with any good relationship!

CHAPTER 9

DISTRIBUTING THE MESSAGE

WHERE: CHANNELS

Even if you have a message you know will connect with your audience, your message is no good if no one sees it! The "If you build it, they will come" philosophy only exists in the movies. In real life people need to know what's going on so they can plan accordingly.

With today's various means of distribution, making sure you know where your audience lives is crucial to monetizing your content and fulfilling your dream. Shows like *Mad Men* glamorize a time when the creative was king. When and where the message was distributed was secondary because there were fewer options and outlets vying for audience attention. You could advertise on television, radio, print, billboards, or signs, but beyond that you were extremely limited in how to reach people.

Today, it's completely different. Not only do you still have all the distribution channels from the *Mad Men* era, but you also have direct mail, experiential marketing, the expansive world of digital media, and much more.

FOR BUSINESSES

It can be difficult to know where to begin if you're just beginning to distribute your story. But fear not, for there are experts in this arena of distribution. Hire a media buyer to help you place your message and content in front of the right audience, or go direct yourself. Just make sure you spend your time and money on the channels that will reach your audience.

As I said previously, times are changing; advertising tactics are too. CEO Kirk Cheyfitz of the international advertising agency Story Worldwide says,

> *The tactics of advertising by intruding in someone's life whether they wanted it or not, that notion is long past. Consumers have taken control of media, and that means something very important. Unless you deliver great media to them that they actually want to watch or hear or read, they have the power to completely ignore you.*

I saw this happen firsthand as a reporter. I saw that telling the story of companies did more for sales than advertising in traditional channels. I was able to go behind the scenes of businesses and tell their unique story in an engaging way. The audience found the story entertaining, and the business saw firsthand the power of a story.

As I continued to receive positive feedback, it fueled my passion for storytelling, and this experience became the springboard for what would eventually become 4th Avenue Media.

Businesses would tell me what a difference their story made for them in sales. Whether I told a story about a national bread company, showing how they made their signature loaves of bread, or featured custom guitars, when a business's story was shared, people listened and responded. Why? Because a story isn't a slick and pretty packaged ad—it is an authentic description that connects emotionally with the right audience, an audience who cares.

Traditional media has done itself a disservice by not keeping current with technology. By rejecting new, digital media channels, traditional media has lost a large portion of their audience. The station I worked at did so by blocking reporters from using Facebook and YouTube (I'm sure they have now removed this rule). The ironic part is, my station touted itself as being "cutting edge." It didn't make sense to say it was "cutting edge" without allowing access to a resource such as YouTube, the 2nd largest search engine in the world, but that's what happened. Once traditional media realized they were the Titanic, it was too late to keep their market share.

PRODUCE YOUR STORY LIKE A PRO

When I was in the newsroom, I began thinking a lot about where the direction of the media—and more specifically where television, advertising, and marketing—was headed. The more I looked into it, the more it all seemed to be converging into digital content. The problem was, most digital content at the time was missing the mark in audience engagement because it didn't look like traditional media. To customers, digital media was too foreign, and people were hesitant to engage with it. Artistic or overly edited videos flooded the internet, but good content was hard to come by. In fact, back in the newsroom we had a disdain for the digital content that was out there at the time because it was so poorly produced.

This transition into the digital age created people who were afraid of being left out of this new platform and were desperate for help and advice. Unfortunately, a lot of people were being misled on how to create and produce digital content. So-called experts were popping up everywhere, trying to convince businesses to use the new digital media, but consumers weren't responding.

I saw this as an opportunity to leave the traditional outlet and drive stronger and more meaningful results for companies. What those so-called experts didn't realize is, people are conditioned to receive content through traditional media outlets such as TV, radio, or print. I used my expertise in how to tell an engaging story in a more traditional format that people were comfortable with, to produce digital content in a way that attracted customers.

Upon moving back to Seattle, I tested my idea of telling a company's story like I would on TV for a friend of mine whose dad was a dentist. I became a "one-man-band" reporter for the dentist's practice. I shot video, interviewed him along with patients, wrote a script, did the voice-over, and edited the story to make it look like it belonged on my feature segment in San Antonio. The result was six new patients the first week the video was on his website. Telling his story was a powerful way to attract customers, and I've since seen it happen over and over again.

WHEN: SCHEDULING

Every person or business with a story needs to start acting like a media station by developing content, distributing content, and tracking who engages with your content in order to monetize your content. Yet this can be difficult to do, and it is one of the biggest problems companies face. The media has the Nielsen ratings, but what does a business have? How are you tracking who's visiting your site, who's seen your ad, or where they heard about you? What are they saying about you? Why do they buy from you? Can you know that exactly? Take heart, because the answer is *yes*.

My answer to this problem is scheduling. No schedule means no monetization, and those who are guilty of not scheduling content are the ones who will tell you that you can't track ROI in social media. But the reason companies don't see direct ROI is because they are going with the "more content is better" model instead of telling people when to expect the content. Focus on quality first, and the quantity will follow.

Tracking the metrics is important in order to see how your content is being received on a daily basis. But don't get too caught up in the daily numbers: look at trends. How are the numbers trending for the week, month, quarter? Building relationships takes time, so don't expect to get huge results from sending out content once.

Create a regularly scheduled content distribution plan, and watch what type of person is engaging with your content. I set up all my clients with a schedule based on content that reflects their unique story and brand. On Facebook, we make sure each day of the week has its own topic, i.e., Mission Mondays, Trending Tuesdays, Event Wednesdays, Throwback Thursdays, and Feature Fridays. After a few weeks, you'll be able to see on Facebook who is engaging with certain posts. When you see a consistent pattern forming, shift all content to what they tune in for most. Not only will this help you build a deeper relationship with your audience, but they will connect with your story and in turn share with others who will connect as well.

You shared. They listened. They shared. You listened.

When scheduling content, don't be afraid to tell your audience loud and clear to tune in. Remember: "People are waiting to be told what to do." It's true, and the media knows it. The stations run promos directing their audience to make an action, and the audience then becomes viewers of content at a specific time.

A large reason this works is because we all live in a systematic, scheduled life. We set our alarms at a certain time, and off we go to work at a certain time. We have watches, phones, and clocks all directing us along our scheduled day. TV stations know that, and that's why they give the same content at the same time, whether daily, weekly, or monthly.

As a reporter, I knew that if someone tuned in at 5:00 PM to watch the news, then we had to deliver what we promised. If we went live at 5:03 PM, then that viewer would not only stop tuning in to our station, but they would go to another station that *did* fulfill the promise of their timeline. That other station would gain a new viewer. If you want to start driving results in achieving your vision, then start acting like a media station: promote your story, and then deliver content around your story at a specific time to your audience. Just make sure to deliver your content at a time that's convenient for your audience. Your audience not only wants it, they expect it!

HOW TO DISTRIBUTE YOUR STORY

Traditional media has conditioned us all, so you have to give people what they want. And what they want is what is most comfortable for them to understand. Whatever channel you use to convey your story, the format of your story must match traditional media in order to get the outcome you are looking for.

One of the most effective types of content to distribute has become video. Video has become the most powerful medium in the online world. It can incorporate text and photos into one highly produced message. But how you produce a video is crucial. And remember, video is just another form of content, so scheduling is equally important for video. Because people are conditioned to watch video through one of two ways—TV and movies—when you produce a video, make sure it's done like one of those two ways, in a style people are already conditioned to watch.

Take eye contact in videos as an example. As video has become such a powerful tool in marketing, it's important to remember that we as an audience and consumers of television are conditioned to allow only three types of people to look at us straight in the eyes: anchors, reporters, and hosts. That's why shows like *The Office* were so groundbreaking when the actors looked straight into the lens to include the audience. The reason this was so impactful was because it was breaking a norm.

You don't have to create broadcast-quality videos to get your message across. Simply producing relevant content and delivering your story in a way that looks and sounds like traditional media will make a positive impact on your audience.

No matter what your dream, delivering your story will bring about a result that otherwise would not be possible. Once you are comfortable delivering your story to others, you will never struggle to navigate through conversations. You will be in control and free to make things happen.

ANOTHER LESSON FROM THE RING

Tactically, here's how you can make sure your audience gets the maximum benefit from your story. First, spend time brainstorming a few months' worth of content, and then take one or two days writing or producing all those stories—yes, just one or two days is all it takes.

For example, let's say you decide to use video as the vehicle to tell your story. You produce short videos full of valuable content that look exactly like you'd see on TV. Schedule all the videos and upload them to a customized YouTube channel that has your company's brand.

From there, track the analytics of the video from YouTube. You want to use this video to drive traffic to other channels, so schedule a time the video will go live

on Facebook. Send out a promo through your email-mar-
keting platform to your audience (your database), telling
them to tune in at the exact time you scheduled your content to go live on Facebook. Then, exactly at the scheduled time, post the video from YouTube to Facebook.
When the video gets posted, be on Facebook, managing
the page, and give incentive with a discount or offer from
your company for the first few people to respond.

The day after the video gets posted to Facebook, archive
the video on your website, providing the value of ongoing
and updated content to your site, which increases your
search engine optimization (SEO). You'll be able to connect with your current audience and give them content
they can share with their friends. This will help your
sales process. Your sales department can send the link of
your stories to the people who watched the video, which
provides value and builds upon the relationship already
established.

The whole plan is to drive the audience to become viewers of your company's Facebook page. This is how you
actually see who is the real audience of your business.
Only you know who should buy from you. By driving the
audience to become specific viewers you can track how
well your marketing plan is working and can see who
actually is buying from your company.

Get the analytics of your Facebook audience and look up
exactly who it is that says they like your programming.

Then you can see that you have, for example, 100 fans on Facebook, but only three people are your demographic and the other 97 are not. Then you focus on the three and ignore the 97. It's the cable model, and it works.

CHAPTER 10

GO FORTH AND BE FREE

GETTING HIT HURTS

Ever watch boxing on TV? I'm always amazed at how watching two men battle toe-to-toe in the ring can look so painless. They'll throw punches to each other, and each punch for the most part doesn't look like it affects the recipient much. In reality the punches do hurt, but each boxer is focused on winning and pushes the feeling of pain out of his mind. He keeps tunnel vision on winning.

You and I are in the ring as well, only our opponent isn't some person laced up with boxing gloves, ready to speed-bag us. Our opponent is called Life, and Life can hit us when we usually least expect it. Life hits us, and if we're not ready, it can feel like it continues to hit us. From this, some people develop a victim mentality and never swing back. They remain stuck in their current state, unhappy, yet unwilling to make a change.

People with a victim mentality never muster up all their strength for one final blow, to knock back at the hits with everything they've got. All people have a choice: either accept the hits and swing back, or try to refuse the hits and cower back into the place where we never had real control over our lives. The difference between the two people is simple: one knows their story and the other doesn't. One braved the questions and stepped out into a place of uncertainty, questioning everything about their own reality to finally come up with what is true, and the other was too afraid of what others would think and so remained stuck.

Don't be the person stuck in the corner. Be free. Be willing. Be a storyteller.

YOUR STORY. YOUR DREAM.

As the Bible says, "Hope deferred makes the heart sick." Without knowing your story, hope for a dream achieved seems only a passing thought as opposed to a living reality. Now that you have read through these chapters, you are equipped not only to know your story but also to be fueled by the passion that comes with your story and fulfill your destiny. Forsake what the naysayers tell you. Go forth and make it happen.

In this book I've taught you four distinct ideas that can and will make your dream a reality. The first step is to develop your authentic story. Question everything. Ask yourself *who*, *what*, *when*, *where*, and *why* about everything you believe until you are able to answer each with passion. After you've questioned and know beyond a shadow of a doubt that the answers you hold as truth, a.k.a. your story, are exactly that, true, be resolute in your beliefs. Begin your journey of fulfilling your dream with passion, courage, and a tenacity that inspires others.

When things don't go exactly the way you planned them to, make sure you're adapting when necessary. The good thing is, when you know your story, you won't falter and quit in the pursuit of your vision. You will only accept the hits and keep going, hopefully avoiding future hits when they come. Your story is everything, because your story is essentially you. It not only acts as the rock to stand on *when* the rain comes and the wind blows, but it also acts as your guide along your journey to fulfilling your vision.

The second step is defining your audience. You need the right people around you; we all do. We can lock arms with people who believe similar things as we do and together, accomplish something far greater than if we go at it alone. The people around us make a huge impact on whether or not we achieve the dreams we have for our lives. This impact can sometimes be in a positive way, but more often than not in a negative way, so choose wisely.

BE BETTER. BE YOU.

I sometimes get asked to speak at schools, and I make sure to give the students one specific message. I ask how many of them have ever heard or said to someone the following question, "Do you think you're better than me?"

I ask them to raise their hands if they've been the recipients of that question. The majority of the hands usually go up. I then ask a follow-up question, "How many of you feel your first reaction is to say *no*?" The majority of the hands still rise. Herein lies the problem to achieving our dreams: fear of our audience rejecting our story.

When we start to make a move toward our dream but haven't fully developed our story, the people surrounding us can viciously turn and ask if we think we're better than them, and because we aren't confidently standing on our story, we say *no* and remain in our state of complacency.

I go on to tell those students what I am telling you now: the next time someone asks the question, "Do you think you're better than me?" Instead of saying *no* and retreating because you don't want to offend anyone, it is alright to say *yes*. It's alright to say, "I am trying to be better than you. I'm trying to be better than me. I'm trying to be *better*. I'm striving for something far greater than my present circumstances, and you are not my standard." It's time to be free from all emotional bondage and guilt and run toward your dream with pure passion and strength.

BOLDNESS LIKE A LION

All this may be new to your way of thinking, but believe me when I say that up until the point when you finally say, "Enough!" to all the naysayers and the negative voices that come from others and inside you, you'll never be free to pursue your dream. Set your sights far above your present circumstances. It's time to be bold. It's time to be free.

Develop your story, choose the right people to be around, and share your story over and over again so you can accomplish what you really want to. Don't settle for someone else's dream. Know your story and settle for nothing less than the vision you have for your life, and you will achieve it.

That's the third step I laid out in this book: distributing your story to your audience in an engaging way that builds a deeper relationship and allows people to connect with you beyond the first time they hear your story. Go a mile deep instead of a mile wide. Share your story and stories about your story in every place where your audience engages with you. The more people who hear and believe the same thing you do, the more people you'll have helping you achieve your dream.

The final step is to benefit from your story—i.e., achieve your dream. Get the results you've always wanted, and help others do the same thing. For the business owner, you can drive the revenue you've always wanted, and for the individual, you'll have the means both internally and externally to continue to move forward when you get hit until you finally cross the finish line and can look back and exclaim, "Victory!"

NEED HELP?

I thank you for reading this book. If I could only do one thing in life, it would be to free every reader by helping them develop their story. Hopefully, you have benefited from reading *Everyone Has a Plan Until They Get Punched in the Face*, and the results will help you thrive in life and business. As you can tell, I am passionate about helping people and businesses develop their unique story. And the truth is, it can be difficult doing it alone. If you would like help in your story development or how to apply it to your marketing, I would be more than happy to work with you.

I also speak at seminars, conferences, and business association meetings. If you would like to book me to speak to your organization or conference email book@4thavenuemedia.com. For more information about my company go to www.4thavenuemedia.com or email info@4thavenuemedia.com.

ABOUT THE AUTHOR

Lucas has always been passionate about inspiring people to strive for something better. He started his professional career at KOMO TV in Seattle as an Audience Coordinator for the live local talk show *Northwest Afternoon*. He then moved to Tri-Cities, Washington, to work as the live Morning Feature Reporter for the NBC affiliate. After spending almost two years there, he moved to San Antonio, Texas, where he was the primary TV Host/ Feature Reporter for the Fox affiliate.

In 2008, Lucas and his family returned to Seattle to work at KOMO TV. In late 2008, Lucas's creative heart won, and he founded 4th Avenue Media with a vision of being the preeminent storytellers in the market. Lucas's years of reporting, producing, writing, branding, and marketing experience fuel his relationships with clients and deliver results that exceed expectations time and time again.

When Lucas isn't working, he is spending cherished time with his family in the Pacific Northwest.